AMERICA AT WAR

Also by Lee Bennett Hopkins

April Bubbles Chocolate: An ABC Book of Poetry

Climb into My Lap: First Poems to Read Together

Hand in Hand: An American History Through Poetry

Happy Birthday

Marvelous Math: A Book of Poems

My America: A Poetry Atlas of the United States

School Supplies: A Book of Poems

Side by Side: Poems to Read Together

Song and Dance

Spectacular Science: A Book of Poems

Wonderful Words: Poems About Reading, Writing, Speaking, and Listening

Yummy! Eating Through a Day

AMERICA AT WAR

Poems selected by LEE BENNETT HOPKINS

Illustrated by
STEPHEN ALCORN

MARGARET K. McELDERRY BOOKS
New York   London   Toronto   Sydney

Special thanks to Charles John Egita for his constant patience and insight; to the many poets whose timeless efforts and edits provided original works to this collection; to Stephen Alcorn for the enthusiasm and dedication he gave to every page of this volume—and to my editor, Emma Dryden, for her ardent devotion.

—L. B. H.

Margaret K. McElderry Books

An imprint of Simon & Schuster Children's Publishing Division

1230 Avenue of the Americas, New York, New York 10020

Text compilation copyright © 2008 by Lee Bennett Hopkins

Illustrations copyright © 2008 by Stephen Alcorn

Book design by Debra Sfetsios

The text for this book is set in Classical Garamond.

The illustrations for this book are rendered in watercolor.

Manufactured in China

10 9 8 7 6 5 4 3 2 1

Library of Congress Cataloging-in-Publication Data

America at war : poems selected by Lee Bennett Hopkins ; illlustrated by Stephen Alcorn.

p. cm.

Includes indexes.

ISBN-13: 978-1-4169-1832-5

ISBN-10: 1-4169-1832-9

1. War poetry, American. 2. United States—History, Military—Poetry. 3. American poetry. I. Hopkins, Lee Bennett. II. Alcorn, Stephen.

PS595.W36A45 2008

811.008'0358—dc22

2006008723

To those . . .

To them . . .

For all of us . . .

— L. B. H.

To my in-laws,

Francesco and Maria,

who as children

in Pisa, Italy,

experienced the tragedy

of war.

— S. A.

Contents

✳✳✳

Introduction

✳ ✳ ✳

America at War is *not* about war. It *is* about the poetry of war. With poems divided into eight sections, warfare is traced from the American Revolution to the Iraqi War via poets' pens. Although I have preceded each section with brief, anecdotal comments, I have not attempted to write the vast history of each war. Libraries contain book after book for readers of all ages, offering time lines, philosophies, firsthand accounts, biographies, pictorial treatments, and so on.

America at War presents raw emotions of warfare as seen and felt by poets—including past masters such as Walt Whitman, Carl Sandburg, and Stephen Crane, as well as over thirty works—more than half of the selections—especially commissioned for this collection. The focus is not solely on the atrocities, bloodshed, and gore that come with battles. What is emphasized is the emotional impact—the torment, grief, and angst that men, women, and children feel as war becomes part of their present-day lives, their future and forever-afters.

We see grief of mothers and fathers, brothers and sisters, who have lost loved ones . . . painfully feeling the same grief, be it in 1775 or today. Through brilliant works of poetry we witness a "mother whose heart hung humble as a button"; a father who gently sits in a pony chair that he and his son carved together, as he weeps for loss; a sister who knows her brother will never dance at her wedding; a brother who so misses a "big-bear/goodnight/hug." We witness a young soldier who wants to be present for the birth of a daughter, another who carries homemade cookies with him to smell home. And we see and feel the effects that war has on children and youth—a boy longing for his mother's voice, a girl "helping to win the war" by depriving herself of common, everyday pleasures.

Throughout the volume Stephen Alcorn's sweeping, dramatic, dynamic artwork serves to add dimension and forethought to the poets' words.

America at War pays fitting tribute to those who have given their lives—or have served us so we may all live in a peace-filled society.

The great American poet Carl Sandburg wrote: "Some day they'll give a war and nobody will come."

If only some day his words will ring true.

LEE BENNETT HOPKINS
Cape Coral, Florida

Prologue

WISH
FOR
PEACE

Joan Bransfield Graham

Would
that war
could only
rage upon the
battlefield of page,
and not a drop of blood
would flow, just ink, and
everyone would know
the word—*freedom*.

THE AMERICAN REVOLUTION
(1775–1783)

"These are the times that try men's souls."

Thomas Paine (1737–1809)
United States Founding Father

The American Revolution began as a result of taxation by the British
without representation of the colonists.

On April 19, 1775, the day after Paul Revere's famous ride, the
"shot heard round the world" was fired at Lexington, Massachusetts, and
colonial Americans and British soldiers then fought for over eight years.

Bloody battles such as those at Bunker Hill in Massachusetts;
Yorktown, Virginia; and Germantown, Pennsylvania, resulted in over
25,000 American fatalities and 10,000 British. At the war's end the
thirteen colonies became the United States of America.

BATTLE OF BUNKER HILL—1775

Ann Whitford Paul

Press on! Press on!
Forget
sweltering sun.
Press on!
Through chain shot,
ring shot, double-headed
shot, falling
thick as hailstones.

Press on!
Shut your ears to the
wounded's piercing groans.
The fear of death
has already left each breast.

Press on!
Descend the hill.
Damn those Redcoats!
Damn those lobsters!
Damn those bloody backs!
Press on! Press on!

STANZAS
Anonymous

Eyes of men running, falling, screaming
Eyes of men shouting, sweating, bleeding
Eyes of the fearful, those of the sad
Eyes of exhaustion and those of the mad.

Eyes of men thinking, hoping, waiting
Eyes of men loving, cursing, hating
Eyes of the wounded sodden in red
Eyes of the dying and those of the dead.

EPITAPH FOR A CONCORD BOY

Stanley Young

Now there is none of the living who can remember
How quietly the sun came into the village of Concord,
No one who will know of the sun in the eyes of the dead boy
There on the village green where he fell.

He did not fall because he hated the Redcoats,
Indeed, he would have known little of them
Had not that quick, grim man, his father,
Hurried him dutifully toward the crackle of musketry.

His father had routed him out and stuck a gun in his hand
And then said something about the "country's deliverance,"
Until the boy went, rubbing the dreams from his eyes
And stood on the green with the others, facing the soldiers.

When the Redcoat leader had shouted, "Disperse, ye rebels,"
The boy would have gone back to his bed willingly,
But as no one else went, he stayed, watching the elegant enemy.
He was never aware the volley of war had been sounded.

GRASS

Carl Sandburg

Pile the bodies high at Austerlitz and Waterloo.
Shovel them under and let me work—
              I am the grass; I cover all.

And pile them high at Gettysburg
And pile them high at Ypres and Verdun.
Shovel them under and let me work.
Two years, ten years, and passengers ask the conductor:

        What place is this?
              Where are we now?

        I am the grass.
        Let me work.

MY SWEET OLD ETCETERA

e. e. cummings

my sweet old etcetera
aunt lucy during the recent

war could and what
is more did tell you just
what everybody was fighting

for,
my sister

isabel created hundreds
(and
hundreds) of socks not to
mention shirts fleaproof earwarmers

etcetera wristers etcetera, my
mother hoped that

i would die etcetera
bravely of course my father used
to become hoarse talking about how it was
a privilege and if only he
could meanwhile my

self etcetera lay quietly
in the deep mud et

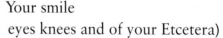

cetera
(dreaming,
et
    cetera, of
Your smile
eyes knees and of your Etcetera)

IN FLANDERS FIELDS

John McCrae

In Flanders fields the poppies blow
Between the crosses row on row
That mark our place; and in the sky
The larks, still bravely singing, fly
Scarce heard amid the guns below.

We are the Dead. Short days ago
We lived, felt dawn, saw sunset glow,
Loved and were loved, and now we lie
In Flanders fields.

Take up our quarrel with the foe:
To you from failing hands we throw
The torch; be yours to hold it high.
If ye break faith with us who die
We shall not sleep, though poppies grow
In Flanders fields.

TWO VOICES

David Westcott Brown

Written May, 1916. Killed 7/14/1916 at Bazentin le Petit
during the Battle of the Somme

'The roads are all torn', 'but the sun's in the sky,'
'The houses are waste'; 'but the day is all fair,'
'There's death in the air'; 'and the larks are on high,'
'Though we die—'; 'It is spring-time, what do we care?'

'The Gardens are rank'; 'but the grass is still green.'
'The orchards are shot-torn'; 'There's bloom on the trees,'
'There's war all around'; 'Yet is nature serene,'
'There's danger'; 'we'll bear it, fanned by the breeze.'

'Some are wounded'; 'they rest, and their glory is known,'
'Some are killed'; 'there's peace for them under the sod,'
'Men's homes are in peril'; 'their souls are their own,'
'The bullets are near us'; 'not nearer than God.'

TROPHY, WW I

Janet Lewis

A cross
I had it from a friend, a Russian woman,
Who found it in a shop in London.
The double cross of Lorraine,
Made of tin, cleverly worked, lusterless,
Set with six bits of glass
Faceted to shine like emeralds,
Inscribed on the back in block letters, lightly scratched,
Verdun.

Verdun, a word to echo
With the sound of guns,
Continual, near, remote, ominous,
The guns of August.
Inscribed also, lightly, the years.
On the lower foot of the cross,
Nineteen-fourteen, nineteen-fifteen, and above,
Above the top crossbar,
Nineteen-sixteen, nineteen-seventeen,
The years of my girlhood.
There is no nineteen-eighteen.

(continued)

The name, hard to decipher,
Begins with an A. Perhaps Audujart,
Of the Seventh Zouaves.
Did he carry it with him
Throughout all those years of cold,
Of stifled fear, and mud,
And endless boredom? Did he make
This cross?

Into whose hands
Was it finally surrendered?
Those of a sweetheart, of a sister,
Of a mother surviving the loss
Of other sons? To be held
Close to the heart, to receive
Warm breath, murmuring a name,
The touch of lips?

No one can speak for it.
In itself it says:
Verdun
And the death of a man.

THERE WILL COME SOFT RAINS

Sara Teasdale

There will come soft rains and the smell of the ground,
And swallows circling with their shimmering sound;

And frogs in the pools singing at night,
And wild plum-trees in tremulous white;

Robins will wear their feathery fire
Whistling their whims on a low fence-wire;

And not one will know of the war, not one
Will care at last when it is done.

Not one would mind, neither bird nor tree
If mankind perished utterly;

And Spring herself, when she woke at dawn,
Would scarcely know that we were gone.

WORLD WAR II
(1939–1945)

*"I think people want peace so much that one of these days
governments had better get out of the way and let them have it."*

Dwight D. Eisenhower (1890–1969)
Thirty-fourth president of the United States

On September 1, 1939, World War II began with Germany invading Poland.
The United States entered the war on December 7, 1941, when Japan
attacked U.S. military bases at Pearl Harbor, Hawaii. The war was fought in
Europe, Asia, the Pacific Islands, and Africa. Seventeen million lives were lost,
including over 400,000 Americans.

A horrific event of this period was the Holocaust, in which German Nazis
organized the murder of over six million Jews—40 percent of the
world's Jewish population—as well as others who questioned Nazism.

When the war ended, the United States became known as
a leading world power.

FRONT PORCH KNITTING

Amy Ludwig VanDerwater

"The men hardly have time to grab their guns before
their wives and sweethearts grab their needles and yarn."
Time/July 21, 1940

Four hands are lit
By full moon glow

Two large
    Two small
Two fast
    Two slow

Hands of mother
Hands of girl

Tightly knit
Neatly purl
Socks for men
In planes
In ditches

Silent prayers
In woolen stitches.

ATLANTIC CITY WARTIME

Nancy Wood

I save fat and string and newspapers. I draw the blackout
curtains each night so enemy submarines
can't see the lights of our house on the beach.

Mama stands in line and buys meat
and sugar with ration stamps. She can't get
coffee or candy bars. I buy Victory bonds
at school and knit Bundles for Britain
out of olive drab yarn. We have a Victory Garden
with corn and beans and tomatoes.

Mama lets out the seams of my too-small dresses
and lines my shoes with cardboard
when they wear out. My father lets me paint
the top half of his headlights black.

I'm helping to win the war.

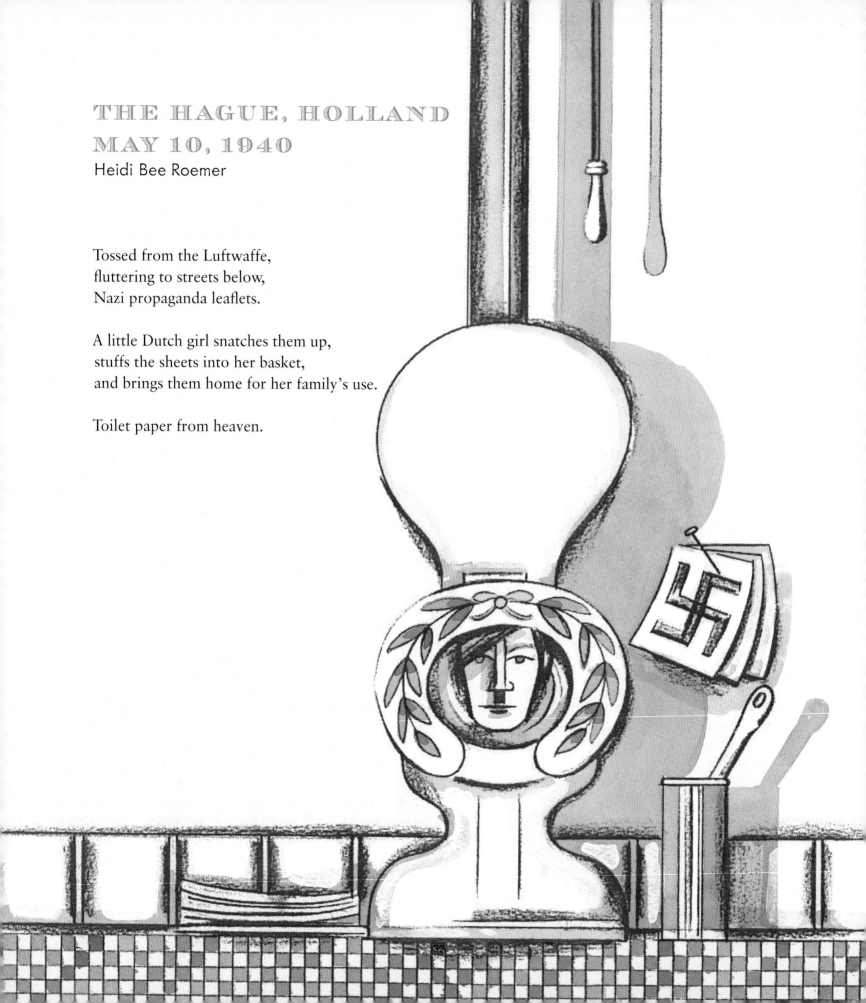

THE HAGUE, HOLLAND
MAY 10, 1940
Heidi Bee Roemer

Tossed from the Luftwaffe,
fluttering to streets below,
Nazi propaganda leaflets.

A little Dutch girl snatches them up,
stuffs the sheets into her basket,
and brings them home for her family's use.

Toilet paper from heaven.

WW II: AMERICAN OCCUPATION, WEINHEIM, GERMANY

Heidi Bee Roemer

for Margarete

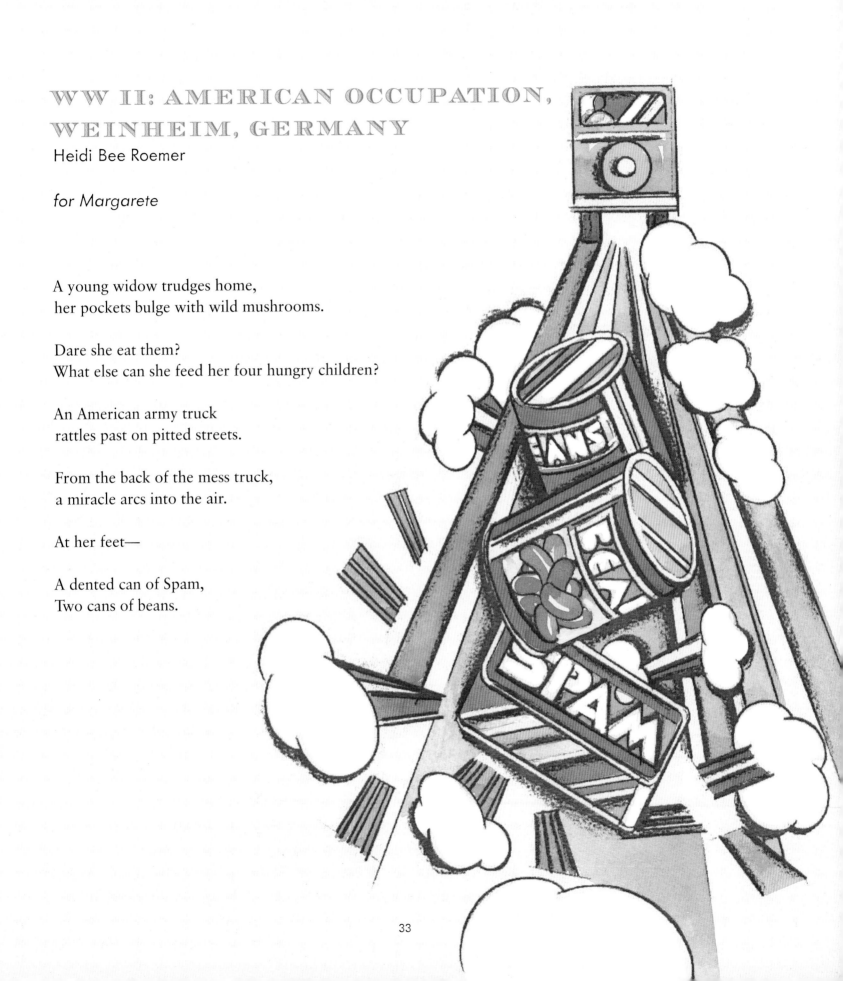

A young widow trudges home,
her pockets bulge with wild mushrooms.

Dare she eat them?
What else can she feed her four hungry children?

An American army truck
rattles past on pitted streets.

From the back of the mess truck,
a miracle arcs into the air.

At her feet—

A dented can of Spam,
Two cans of beans.

AS I DO NOW

Katie McAllister Weaver

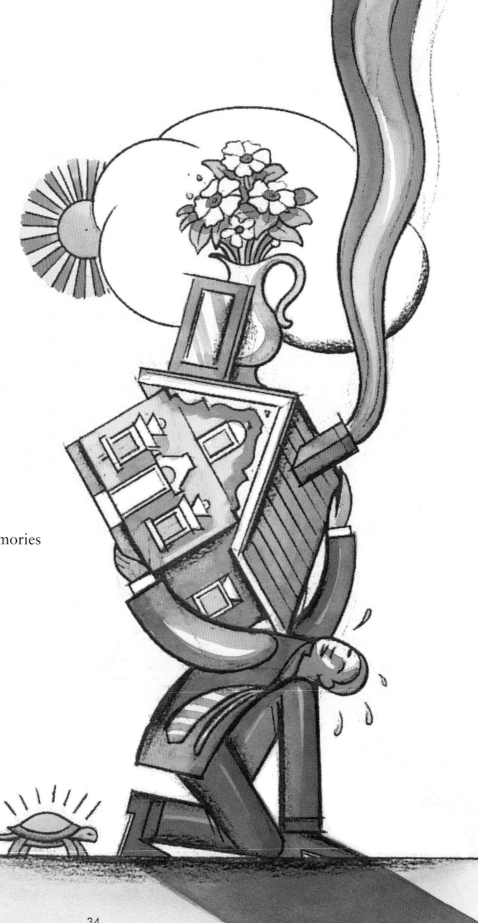

We were told to take
only what was too important
to leave behind

Even frantic rantings
of our neighbors fleeing screams
couldn't help us decide.

The relentless threat of Nazis
muddled our every thought—
again,
a night like
> KRISTALLNACHT!

We grabbed what we could carry.
Yet, eventually favorite photos,
stacks of books, mounting piles of memories
lined roadsides like gravestones
until all we had left
were backpacks of food
and the weight of wishing
we could have brought more.

My small crystal turtle, though,
stashed under my shirt
reminded me how
I never needed it
as much as I do now.

ALPHABET

Jane Yolen

What is the alphabet of evil?
Auschwitz,
Buchenwald,
Chelmno,
the names of camps,
rolling off the tongue,
the tongue lolling in the mouth,
the mouth hanging open,
broken teeth,
a gasp of breath,
the alphabet of death.

What is the alphabet of evil?
Dachau,
Esterwegen,
Flossenberg,
Gurs,
the names of camps
cramping the stomach,
the stomach drained of blood,
blood, staining the ground,
a last breath,
the alphabet of death.

(continued)

What is the alphabet of evil?
It begins with Adolph Hitler,
goes to the Zondercommandos
ends with the ordinary citizen
turning in his neighbor,
a sheckle for a traitor,
a groat for a Jew.

What is the alphabet of evil?
Small letters
we all know how to say,
and hope we are never asked
in our ordinary lives
to say them.

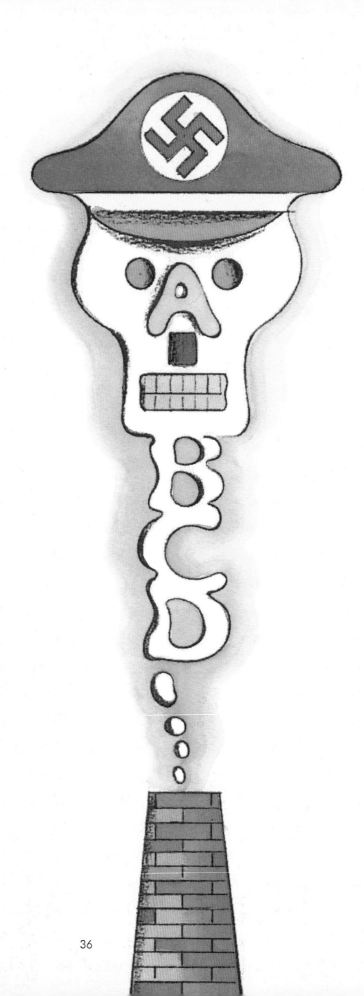

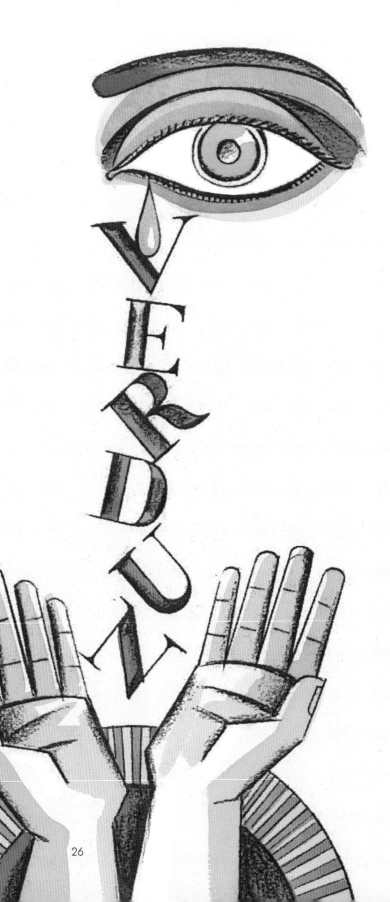

ONCE MORE

Lee Bennett Hopkins

for C. J. E.

Outside the church
I wait.
Wait for someone
anyone
to invite me
for a longing
Christmas dinner.

No one does.

The cheap hotel room
I'm in
on leave
is dank
dark
grim—
not a trace
of angels
snow
a star-lit tree
a manger
a nativity.

Just a lamp
a bed
a phone
a lonely me.

(continued)

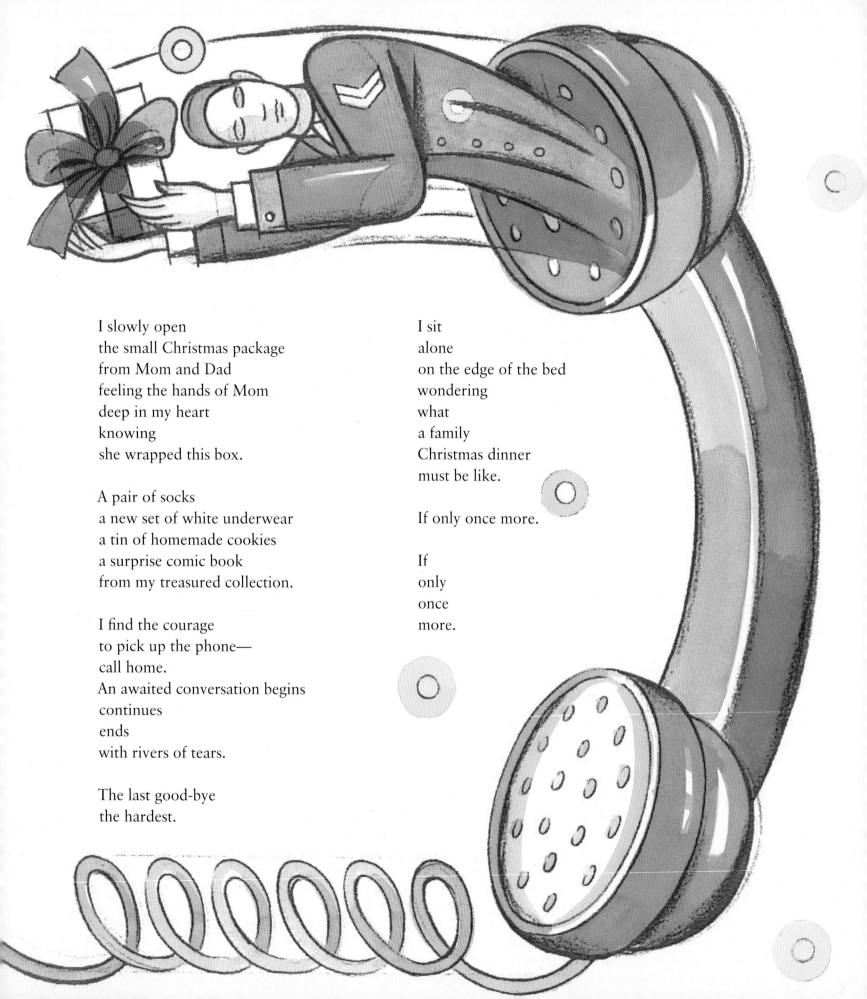

I slowly open
the small Christmas package
from Mom and Dad
feeling the hands of Mom
deep in my heart
knowing
she wrapped this box.

A pair of socks
a new set of white underwear
a tin of homemade cookies
a surprise comic book
from my treasured collection.

I find the courage
to pick up the phone—
call home.
An awaited conversation begins
continues
ends
with rivers of tears.

The last good-bye
the hardest.

I sit
alone
on the edge of the bed
wondering
what
a family
Christmas dinner
must be like.

If only once more.

If
only
once
more.

AMERICA'S WELCOME HOME
Henry Van Dyke

Oh, gallantly they fared forth in khaki and in blue,
America's crusading host of warriors bold and true;
They battled for the rights of man beside our brave Allies,
And now they're coming home to us with glory in their eyes.

Oh, it's home again, and home again. America for me!
Our hearts are turning home again and there we long to be,
In our beautiful big country beyond the ocean bars,
Where the air is full of sunlight and the flag is full of stars.

Our boys have seen the Old World as none have seen before.
They know the grisly horror of the German gods of war:
The noble faith of Britain and the hero-heart of France,
The soul of Belgium's fortitude and Italy's romance.

They bore our country's great word across the rolling sea,
"America swears brotherhood with all the just and free."
They wrote that word victorious on fields of mortal strife,
And many a valiant lad was proud to seal it with his life.

Oh, welcome home in Heaven's peace, dear spirits of the dead!
And welcome home ye living sons America hath bred!
The lords of war are beaten down, your glorious task is done;
You fought to make the whole world free, and the victory is won.

Now it's home again, and home again, our hearts are turning west,
Of all the lands beneath the sun America is best.
We're going home to our own folks, beyond the ocean bars,
Where the air is full of sunlight and the flag is full of stars.

KOREAN WAR
(1950–1953)

"War does not determine who is right—
only who is left."

Bertrand Russell (1872–1970)
British philosopher

Communist-ruled North Korea invaded South Korea to gain control of
the entire country. The United Nations demanded withdrawal. Orders were
ignored, causing the U.N. to engage in its first military role since its 1945
establishment. The United States entered the war under the banner of
the U.N., along with fifteen allied countries who sent troops and supplies
to help the South Koreans.

In just three years deaths numbered 2,500,000; American casualties
amounted to 103,000.

The irony of this war is that no one won. Korea remains divided to this day.

NOT A WAR
Bruce Balan

Korea, that is.
Not a war, *officially*.
Never declared.
Instead,
Only a police action.
Two and a half million soldiers
Dead.
Not a war.

And the civilians?
Cut down by crossfire,
Bombed in their beds.

We can't say:
"Oh well,
War is hell."

No.
Try to tell Su-mi
And Jung-hwa and Yoon-hee
And two million others
Who are no more.

Sorry.
Very sorry.

Not a war.

from

CHILDREN AND WAR

John Sullivan

III

father an infantryman
has children sing happy birthday
to his photo

GRAVEYARD

Rebecca Kai Dotlich

It is settled then.

This is where
you will sleep.

This is where
while I grow old,
you will not.

This is where
I will tell you secrets.
Where I will never
hear yours.

This is where
we've ended:

You, my soldier.
I, your sister.

You will never
fall in love.

You will never
dance at my wedding.

TWO SIDES OF A COIN

Betsy Franco

When I was six,
I remember my father's
dark blue Navy uniform,
when we visited the ship
where he worked
in Yokosuka harbor.

I remember learning
to fold paper cranes;
playing tag with farm children
who chased me
with chicken feathers
and spoke only Japanese.

I remember staring at
the giant sandals
of the great Buddha statue
in the Japanese city where we lived—
during two years
of the Korean War.

(continued)

It wasn't until much later as a teenager
that I found out my father's job
was to repair soldiers shipped back
from Korea because their jaws
were shot up
or completely shattered.

"I can see it like it was yesterday,"
my father would say.
"Let's talk about something else."

from

MARKINGS
Dag Hammarskjöld

I ask: what am I doing here?
And, at once, this *I*
Becomes unreal.

VIETNAM WAR
(1957–1975)

". . . wars have a way of going on and on
in your mind and your soul
long after you've left the
battlefield."

Philip Caputo (1941–   )
Marine lieutenant &
Pulitzer Prize–winning journalist

The United States became involved in the Vietnam War in 1961, when it was feared that if Vietnam were to fall under Communist rule, the rest of Asia would follow. A cease-fire was arranged in January 1973; American ground troops left Vietnam. Fighting began again, but U.S. troops did not return.

The Vietnam War was viewed as an "unpopular war"; many Americans felt that U.S. involvement was cruel and unnecessary. The United States suffered 58,000 deaths.

from

MYTHS OF GLORY

John Kent,
United States Marine Corps

1

The orphan boy
has one arm,
he stares at me
from the side of the road;
a lifetime of hate
in eight short years.

4

The Saigon street
is filled with people,
the sound of life energizing,
the business of living
intensely pursued.
A shell explodes, then another
and another.
The Saigon street
is filled with the sounds of death.

11

There is a place called home.
I don't know where that is.

CHARMS
Georgia Heard

Soldiers stuck the ace of spades into helmet bands,
lugged Bibles through jungles in backpacks,
cradled Mezuzahs, locks of hair, crumpled photos
of John F. Kennedy, Martin Luther King, the Pope,
the Beatles, in camouflage pockets. Crosses,
St. Christophers dangled from strong necks,
resting against fearful hearts.
They slept with creased snapshots of families,
wives, kids, dogs, clutched tightly in their fists.

One soldier even carried a homemade oatmeal cookie
his entire tour of Vietnam, swaddled in tin foil.

When he was homesick
        he unwrapped it,
            held it up to his nose,
                to smell
                    what home
                        was like.

KILROY

Eugene McCarthy

Kilroy is gone,
the word is out,
absent without leave
from Vietnam.

Kilroy
who wrote his name
in every can
from Poland to Japan
and places in between
like Sheboygan and Racine
is gone
absent without leave
from Vietnam.

Kilroy
who kept the dice
and stole the ice
out of the BOQ
Kilroy whose name was good
on every IOU
in World War II
and even in Korea
is gone
absent without leave
from Vietnam.

Kilroy
the unknown soldier
who was the first to land
the last to leave,
with his own hand
has taken his good name
from all the walls
and toilet stalls.

Kilroy
whose name around the world
was like the flag unfurled
has run it down
and left Saigon
and the Mekong
without a hero or a song
and gone
absent without leave
from Vietnam.

WHISPERS TO THE WALL

Rebecca Kai Dotlich

You are him, from Maine,
him, from Montana,
and every him from sea
to sea and back.

Stewart, Kelly, York:
you are all of those
who shrimped on boats,
flew planes,
studied, wrote,
collected,
kissed.

The brave ones spill
across your face;
an indelible trace
of young sons
who played baseball,
cards, guitars.

Thompson, Sanchez, Vance:
you know their favorite dish,
their first romance.
On silent nights, do they tell you
of boyhoods and Beatles,
bruised knees and hearts,
birthdays missed . . .
those who shrimped on boats,
flew planes
studied, wrote,
collected,
kissed?

WAR IS THE FIERCEST ART

Sara Holbrook

The Luc Bat poet knew
His country broke in two, therefore
He had to go to war.
His wife and child, heartsore, waved bye.
The poet dared not cry.
He needed a clear eye to spill
Blood, strangers he must kill
To stay alive until the time
He could again in rhyme
Make images sublime. His heart
Was wracked, torn apart.
War is the fiercest art. Trading
Pen for gun, evading
Death, armies invading. This hate
Was not his normal state.
One question would frustrate, for he
Knew not this enemy.

"Might you write poetry?
I, too."

WHAT WERE THEY LIKE?
Denise Levertov

1) Did the people of Vietnam
   use lanterns of stone?
2) Did they hold ceremonies
   to reverence the opening of buds?
3) Were they inclined to quiet laughter?
4) Did they use bone and ivory,
   jade and silver, for ornament?
5) Had they an epic poem?
6) Did they distinguish between speech and singing?

1) Sir, their light hearts turned to stone.
   It is not remembered whether in gardens
   stone lanterns illumined pleasant ways.
2) Perhaps they gathered once to delight in blossom,
   but after the children were killed
   there were no more buds.
3) Sir, laughter is bitter to the burned mouth.
4) A dream ago, perhaps. Ornament is for joy.
   All the bones were charred.
5) It is not remembered. Remember,
   most were peasants, their life
   was in rice and bamboo.
   When peaceful clouds were reflected in the paddies
   and the water buffalo steeped surely along terraces,
   maybe fathers told their sons old tales.
   When bombs smashed those mirrors
   there was time only to scream.
6) There is no echo yet
   of their speech which was like a song.
   It was reported their singing resembled
   the flight of moths in moonlight.
   Who can say? It is silent now.

VIETNAM
Linda Ellsworth Crisalli

I play in my backyard
secretly killing
invisible enemies
with my forbidden
toy gun
to make

sure
you come home.

I crawl through jungles
of lawn chairs
over seas of grass
coiled snakes
of garden hose.

I slip into
woodshed darkness.

I aim and fire
over and over again
at faceless fears.
I shout your name.

Hide my toy
in our old magnolia tree.

Go into
the house.

Sit down
to dinner.

from

CHILDREN AND WAR

John Sullivan

VII
veterans memorial
touching the name of a man
who was like his twin

PERSIAN GULF WAR
(1991)

"We make war that we may live in peace."
Aristotle (384–322 B.C.)
Greek philosopher

On August 2, 1990, Iraqi forces invaded and seized control of Kuwait
to take over the country's rich oil fields and gain access to the Persian
Gulf. Immediately the United Nations declared the invasion an illegal act,
demanding Iraq's withdrawal from Kuwait.

On January 16, 1991, a U.S. military campaign, Operation Desert Storm,
began. Iraq surrendered after forty-five days. During the brief period
147 Americans died and 467 were wounded.

WATCHING KUWAIT OIL FIRES ON TV

Ann Wagner

It's as if some artist with a charcoal stick
drew plumes of dark rising,
billowy and thick,
spreading across a canvas of sky.

I watch birds struggling in slick, oily rain,
flames flaring up
in bright bursts of pain—
the only color in the dying land.

There's no other light
TV cameras succumb
to the smothering night
as it reaches down to a burnt-crust shore

and shrouds my screen with the blackness of war.

DESERT STORM
Terri Cohlene

On TV
everything is preempted
by Desert Storm.

You see
far away oil fields burning
far away missiles flying—
over Baghdad, Kuwait, Israel.

Far away
gas masks come
in children's sizes.

What started it all?
Oil. Power.
Who has it?
Who wants it?
Who takes it?
Who will end it?

Suddenly it is over.
You return
to scheduled programming.

ARMS
Janet Settimo

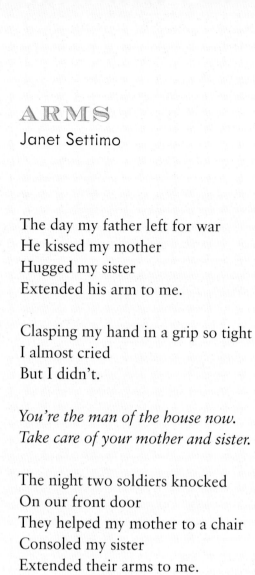

The day my father left for war
He kissed my mother
Hugged my sister
Extended his arm to me.

Clasping my hand in a grip so tight
I almost cried
But I didn't.

You're the man of the house now.
Take care of your mother and sister.

The night two soldiers knocked
On our front door
They helped my mother to a chair
Consoled my sister
Extended their arms to me.

You're the man of the house now.
Make your father proud.

The morning of the service
After the final eulogy
The flag was folded
Into a small tight triangle
And placed in my mother's arms

But my arms are empty.

I'm the man of the house now.

MISSING
Cynthia Cotten

My brother is a soldier
in a hot, dry,
sandy place.
He's missing—
missing things like
baseball, barbecues,
fishing, French fries,
chocolate sodas,
flame-red maple trees,
blue jays,
and snow.

I'm missing, too—
missing
his read-out-loud voice,
his super-special
banana pancakes,
his scuffed up shoes
by the back door,
his big-bear
good night
hug.

There are people
with guns
in that land of sand
who want to shoot
my brother.

I hope
they miss him,
too.

MY BROTHER'S SHIRT
Rebecca Kai Dotlich

It is mine now,
one stiff army shirt,
THOMPSON printed
on the pocket.
United States Army
sends something home;
gives part of you back.
The part that cannot
breathe, or speak
or tease me
anymore.

IRAQ WAR
(2001–　)

"One minute we're trying to catch a fly ball,
the next minute, we're praying
not to get blown into
a million pieces."

Staff Sergeant Dawayne Harterson
Camp Warhorse, Iraq, 2005
Company A/467th Engineer Battalion

And so . . . still . . . another war.

        Ring around a rosy,

        A pocket full of posy,

        Ashes . . .

            Ashes . . .

                All fall down.

CARE PACKAGE

Janet Settimo

The box is heavy
as I stand in line
at the post office but
I don't mind because
this box—
this care package
is addressed to my sister.

I imagine her smile as
she opens the box to find
cherry-flavored lip balm
spicy beef jerky
pre-moistened baby wipes
(she can be a baby at times)
lavender hand cream
and snapshots of
my summer sleepover.

I imagine my sister's smile as
the clerk says, "Next."
I place the package on the counter.

"What is the value of the contents?"
"Not much," I say. *Priceless*, I think.
"And if we can't locate this soldier?
Would you like the package returned to you,
given to another soldier, or abandoned?"

I'm stunned into silence.
I'm imagining my sister's smile . . .

"Miss?" the clerk repeats.

"Give it to another soldier," I say softly.
But my heart is screaming find her.

FIND HER!

A SOLDIER'S LETTER TO A NEWBORN DAUGHTER

Joan Bransfield Graham

How I wanted to be
    there
to hear your
    first cry—
they say you have your
    mother's eyes.
I've looked
    at your picture
a thousand times—
    made my buddies
look, too—I'm
    proud of you.
I long to hold you,
    kiss your head,
rock you to sleep,
    but for now
I can only
    keep you in a
pocket,
    close to my heart.
You're finally
    HERE—I'm so *glad*!
I'm coming home
    to my girls . . .

       With All My Love,
       DAD

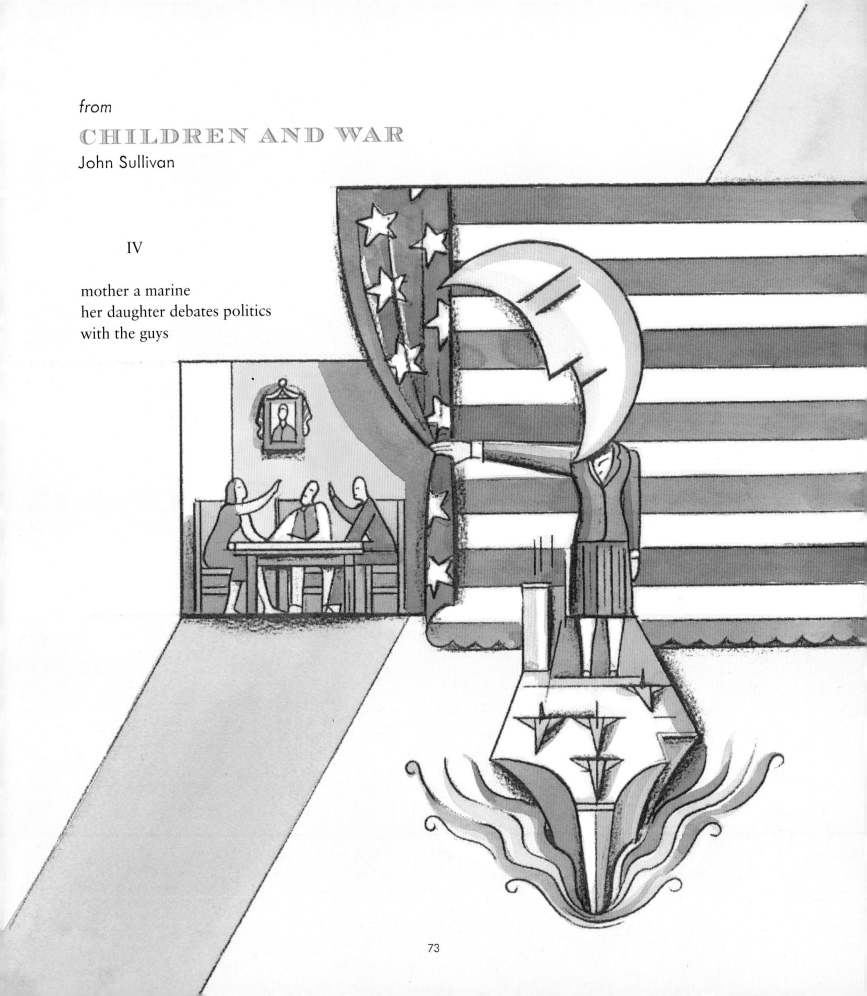

from

CHILDREN AND WAR

John Sullivan

IV

mother a marine
her daughter debates politics
with the guys

TO YOU
Karla Kuskin

I think I could walk
through the simmering sand
if I held your hand.
I think I could swim
the skin-shivering sea
if you would accompany me.
And run on ragged, windy heights,
climb rugged rocks
and walk on air:

I think I could do anything at all,
if you were there.

from

MECHANICAL BIRDS
Denver Butson

today
  let's
forget
  to
remember
  how
slain
  our
hearts
  will
  be
when
  it's
  over

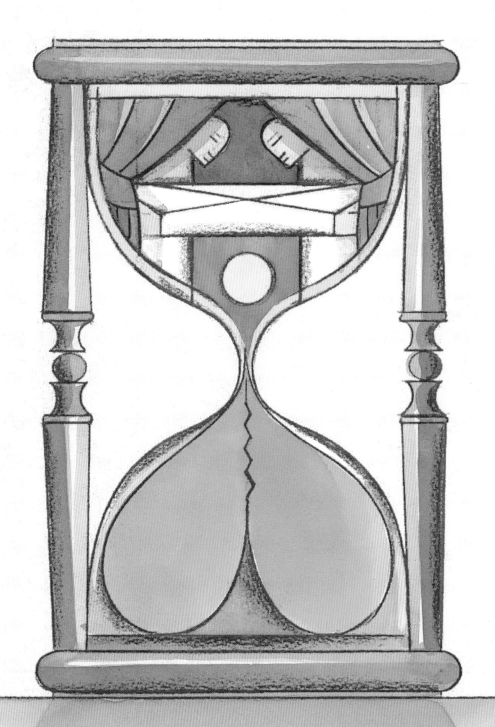

A SMALL TOWN MOURNS ITS FIRST CASUALTY

Ben Myers

No parade today.
Our small town sulks
in uneasy innocence.
Today birds sing dirges
to widowed willows
to silence
settled on weeping streets.
Buildings are hollow
with no soul left
behind their brownstone bodies.
Barber chairs stand in line, empty;
the glass-faced diner, squatting
on Main Street, is only
a scent of memory.
Today the sky is wrapped
in the shroud of Heaven's flag.

A small town mourns its first casualty.

DREAMS

Langston Hughes

Hold fast to dreams
For if dreams die
Life is a broken-winged bird
That cannot fly.

Hold fast to dreams
For when dreams go
Life is a barren field
Frozen with snow.

Epilogue

VOCABULARY LESSON

Ann Wagner

We don't have wars.

We have

conflicts
campaigns
operations
escalations
missions
offensives
preemptive strikes.

We don't have soldiers.

We have

peace keepers
troops
servicemen
servicewomen
forces
coalitions
units.

We don't have mistakes in combat.

We have

       incidents
       accidents
       friendly fire
       flawed intelligence.

And we don't have death.

We have

       casualties
       loss of life
       collateral damage.

What we do have is

       a careful vocabulary.

Acknowledgments

Every effort has been made to trace the ownership of all copyrighted material and to secure necessary permissions to reprint these selections. In the event of any questions arising as to the use of any material, the editor and the publisher, while expressing regret for any inadvertent error, will be happy to make the necessary correction in future printings. Thanks are due to the following for permission to reprint the selections below:

Bruce Balan for "Not a War." Used by permission of the author, who controls all rights. ● Denver Butson for a verse from *Mechanical Birds*. Used by permission of the author, who controls all rights. ● Terri Cohlene for "Desert Storm." Used by permission of the author, who controls all rights. ● Cynthia Cotten for "Drummer" and "Missing." Used by permission of the author, who controls all rights. ● Linda Ellsworth Crisalli for "Vietnam." Used by permission of the author, who controls all rights. ● Curtis Brown, Ltd. for "Graveyard" and "My Brother's Shirt." Copyright 2008 by Rebecca Kai Dotlich; "Whispers to the Wall" by Rebecca Kai Dotlich. Copyright © 2005 by Rebecca Kai Dotlich. First appeared in *A Kick in the Head*, published by Candlewick Press. ● "Once More" by Lee Bennett Hopkins. Copyright © 2008 by Lee Bennett Hopkins; "Alphabet" by Jane Yolen. Copyright © 2008 by Jane Yolen. All reprinted by permission of Curtis Brown, Ltd. ● Betsy Franco for "Two Sides of a Coin." Used by permission of the author, who controls all rights. ● Joan Bransfield Graham for "A Soldier's Letter to a Newborn Daughter" and "Wish for Peace." Used by permission of the author, who controls all rights. ● Harcourt, Inc. for "Grass" from *The Complete Poems of Carl Sandburg*, copyright © 1970, 1969 by Lilian Steichen Sandburg, Trustee, reprinted by permission of Harcourt, Inc. ● Georgia Heard for "Charms." Used by permission of the author, who controls all rights. ● Sara Holbrook for "War Is the Fiercest Art." Used by permission of the author, who controls all rights. ● Tony Johnston for "The Pony Chair." Used by permission of the author, who controls all rights. ● J. Patrick Lewis for "Letter Home, July, 1864." Used by permission of the author, who controls all rights. ● Liveright Publishing Corporation for "my sweet old etcetera." Copyright 1926, 1954, © 1991 by the Trustees for the e. e. cummings Trust. Copyright © 1985 by George James Firmage from *Complete Poems: 1904–1962* by e. e. cummings, edited by George J. Firmage. Used by permission of Liveright Publishing Corporation. ● Beverly McLoughland for "The Whippoorwill Calls." Used by permission of the author, who controls all rights. ● Ben Myers for "A Small Town Mourns Its First Casualty." Used by permission of the author, who controls all rights. ● New Directions Publishing Corporation for "What Were They Like?" from *Poems 1960–1967* by Denise Levertov. Copyright © 1966 by Denise Levertov. Reprinted by permission of New Directions Publishing Corp. ● Ann Whitford Paul for "Battle of Bunker Hill—1775." Used by permission of the author, who controls all rights. ● Brenda Powelson-Vick for "Brother Against Brother." Used by permission of the author, who controls all rights. ● Random House, Inc. for "Dreams" and "Youth" from *The Collected Poems of Langston Hughes* by Langston Hughes. Copyright © 1994 by The Estate of Langston Hughes. Used by permission of Alfred A. Knopf, a division of Random House, Inc. ● Heidi Bee Roemer for "The Hague, Holland—May 10, 1940" and "WW II: American Occupation—Weinheim, Germany—For Margarete." Used by permission of the author, who controls all rights. ● Janet Settimo for "Arms" and "Care Package." Used by permission of the author, who controls all rights. ● John Sullivan for "Children and War—III, IV, VII." Used by permission of the author, who controls all rights. ● Swallow Press/Ohio State University for "Trophy, WW I" from *The Selected Poems of Janet Lewis*, by Janet Lewis, edited by R. L. Barth, 2000. Reprinted with the permission of Swallow Press/Ohio University Press, Athens, Ohio. ● Scott Treimel for "To You" by Karla Kuskin. Copyright © 1987 by Karla Kuskin. Used by permission of Scott Treimel, NY. ● Amy Ludwig VanDerwater for "Front Porch Knitting." Used by permission of the author, who controls all rights. ● Ann Wagner for "Vocabulary Lesson" and "Watching Kuwait Oil Fires on TV." Used by permission of the author, who controls all rights. ● Katie McAllister Weaver for "As I Do Now." Used by permission of the author, who controls all rights. ● Nancy Wood for "Atlantic City Wartime." Used by permission of the author, who controls all rights.

Index of Authors

Index of Titles

Index of First Lines